Mona,
My pastor wrote ... me this ... ...ing
this book for ...
in his congr...
book was me
especially since &
& then your surgery.
mine now.

Sept. '09

# FEEL GOOD ABOUT LIFE...

# AGAIN

# FEEL GOOD
# ABOUT LIFE...
# AGAIN

## Rick McDaniel

# Acknowledgements

No significant work can be done without a team of people. I am blessed to be surrounded by a staff that really helps me to do all the work God has directed me to do. On this project I have been especially helped by Matt McGhan with graphics and layout. Anthony Burns has been a great benefit coordinating everything with CreateSpace and Amazon. My outstanding assistant Dianna Smith-Miller has done her usual excellent work of keeping me on track and focused. Finally, my marvelous wife Michelle continues to support me in all my varied endeavors.

# CONTENTS

# FAITH
# OR
# FEAR

All you have to do is look at today's front page of the newspaper or turn on the nightly news and all you see is "Foreclosures are up, the stock market is down, and more jobs have been lost." Everywhere you look there are challenging problems facing our world. A worldwide recession has caused untold misery for many people and caused almost everyone to not feel good about life. This book is not about how those giant problems can be solved but it is about how you can personally respond to what is happening in your life. It is about how you can feel good about life again.

The greatest power in life that a person possesses is the power to choose. Life is 10% what happens to you and 90% how you respond to what happens to you. You can't control the economy and neither can I. However, you can control yourself, you can control your attitude, you can control your emotions, you can control your outlook. You can choose faith or fear. Don't give in to fear. Just don't do it! Fear is spreading and it is spreading throughout this country and world. It is spreading and it is a bad thing that you need to change for yourself. When you give in to fear, you do nothing to help yourself and you do many things that can harm yourself and harm your future. You have got to fight against the negativity in your own mind and the negativity that is surrounding you. Depending on how you choose you can actually have the most exciting year of your life. This year has incredible potential, depending on how you approach it.

You have just gotten too much of a steady diet of negativity and bad news and it is causing you to be fearful and afraid. You may have to stop talking to some of your friends because some of your friends are so negative, are so filled with anxiety and fear that they are passing it along to you. Here is what I know and have experienced for years: tough times never last, tough people do. This too shall pass, this will be gone, it will be over. But how you respond to this challenge is going to define you. And it is going to set you on one direction or another for the future in your life. I believe that pressure doesn't make the person it reveals the person. How you respond to this tough environment, this tough economic situation is huge for you. You control your response to what is happening. You choose whether to feel good about life again or not. What I can tell you is that God has always provided and He always will. To those who claim to be followers of Christ, this is your finest hour to show what you say you believe. If we are people of Faith, then it is now time to exercise that faith. Are you going to stand strong in challenging times or are you going to give in to anxiety and fear?

In Mark 9: 21-24 it says, "Jesus asked the boy's father, "How long has he been like this?" The man answered, "Ever since he was a child. The demon has often tried to kill him by throwing him into fire or into water. Please have pity on us and help us if you can." Jesus replied, "Why do you say if you can? Anything is possible for someone who has faith." Right away, the boy's father shouted, "I do have faith! Please help me to have even more." Maybe you feel like the boy's father, you need God's help right now to have faith greater than your fear. Fear is a challenge that has faced human beings from the start. In the Bible, from the beginning of it to the end you read things like this: "Don't be fearful." "Don't be afraid." "Don't be anxious." "Be bold." "Be courageous." The Bible challenges you because the Bible knows human beings are prone to be afraid. This is a fearful time and the challenge before you is: are you going to give into fear or not?

Jesus said in John 10:10 "I came that you might have life and have it abundantly." Jesus wants you to have an abundant life, which literally means a life of surplus. Steven Covey coined the phrase "abundance mentality" which is a good description of the way Jesus wants you to think about life. Scarcity mentality means that you see life and resources as limited. It is as if there is a pie and it is only so big so you have to protect your piece of the pie because there is only so much pie to go around. Abundance mentality challenges the belief that the pie is only that big. It says that maybe the pie is much bigger so that there is plenty for everyone. If the pie is bigger and the sizes of the pieces are the same, then there is a giant difference in how much is left over. God makes big pies. You are not living in some small little scarce world of resources. God has all that you need. If you look at your life from a scarcity mentality you are going directly opposite of all that the Bible teaches of what a follower of Christ looks like. We are people who give, we are people who share, we are people who believe that God provides. Where God guides God provides. I have seen it over and over again in my own life and in many people's lives. You have to have an abundance mentality in which you believe that God has plenty for everyone. You don't have to live your life protecting your little piece fearful that somebody else might take it. You have got to think in terms of how it is that fear breeds a scarcity mentality and how that mentality goes directly against what God wants for your life. You need to welcome in what Jesus said about the abundant life that He has for you. Whatever it is you need God can provide it for you and now it is time to test your faith! If you claim to be a follower of Christ, this is your greatest hour to actually put into practice what you claim to believe.

What I know about fear is that it is limiting and none of us can afford any more limitations. We have got enough limitations happening already in our lives. There are plenty of things you can't control but you can control your approach to the challenges you are facing. Fear will limit you; it will keep you from God's best. A characteristic of fear is that it is emotionally draining. When you are drained emotionally, you can't be hopeful. Giving in to challenges and difficulties will cause you to go negative and that is absolutely the wrong direction to go. It is so easy to do that and many people are doing it, but it is not the right way to go. That approach is not going to help you, it is not going to bless you, it is not going to move you where you need to be.

God has not given you a spirit, a mentality of fearfulness. That is not what God wants for your life. You look around and see all these bad things and I don't deny the reality of them. My challenge is what good does it do for you to give in when God has something better, which you never would have been open to unless you go through these kind of challenging times. Tough times, challenging times, difficult times cause us to rethink things; cause us to be open in ways we are not open to if things are going the way we want them to go. And it is in those times that God can direct or redirect your life. It is in those times that God can show you things that you wouldn't see because you wouldn't have been looking for them. Unfortunately, many times God gets your attention through difficult times. I believe you may be prone to keep things the way they are unless enough pain comes into your life to make you change.

There are many people who have not lost their jobs and other financial resources. Their paycheck hasn't changed and their expenses haven't really changed that much either. Their 401K might be different, the value of their home might be different, but their day to day expenses have not really changed and yet according to ABC News they have cut back their spending by 20-25%. Why is that happening? It is happening because of fear, scarcity mentality, and lack of faith.

So here is the challenge for you. Will you live by fear or faith? What is it going to be? You can make fear based decisions or you can make faith based decisions. You will look back on those faith based decisions and you will see how God provided, and you will be so pleased that you put your trust in God and did not give into fear. Those faith based decisions will result in things happening that you have never seen before. You will learn more about yourself than ever before and you will have new opportunities open up before you.

# KEEP STRESS FROM BECOMING DISTRESS

Not all stress is bad, you need a certain amount of stress in your life in order to perform tasks, to get things done and to achieve your goals. But when stress is excessive or is extended over a period of time, it can become distress. It then becomes very negative for your physical and emotional health. There is a difference between stress that you have to live with and work with and distress, which is extended stress.

Let me share seven myths about stress that come from two doctors, Everly and Rosenfeld, in a book called *The Nature and Treatment of the Stress Response*. The first is that stress-related symptoms are all in your head, and therefore they can't really injure you. The second is that only weak people suffer from stress. The third myth says that you are not responsible for the stress in your life. Stress is unavoidable these days so we are all victims. The fourth suggests that you always know when you begin to suffer from excessive stress. The reality is that you don't always recognize the onset of stress. The fifth myth says that it is easy to identify the causes of excessive stress. The sixth myth says that all people respond to stress in the same way. The seventh myth is that when you begin to suffer from excessive stress, all you have to do is sit down and relax. Oh, if it were only that easy. These myths have been identified by doctors who have treated stress and stress-related injuries and illnesses, so they understand something about the reality of stress and its negative impact on your life. You need to understand how you can overcome it and deal with it.

## Symptoms of Stress

There is a story in the Bible about Elijah in I Kings 19:1-26 where you see some universal symptoms of stress. The issue in his life was one of intense pressure from stress - stress that can lead to distress. You might think, that some story about a bearded, robe-wearing prophet living on the other side of the world, three thousand years ago, has nothing to do with your modern day stress. You will see from this story how insightful and helpful the Bible is to the challenges of stress.

### Depreciate Your Worth

The first symptom of stress is that you depreciate your own worth. "I have had enough, Lord. Take my life," Elijah says in verse four. When you have reached a place of depreciating your self worth to its extreme, you have those kinds of suicidal thoughts. You think, "I am better off dead than alive. My life is so difficult, so burdensome that I would rather be dead than to keep living the way I am living now." Depressive moods will cause you to not think clearly about your true value to yourself and others.

### Underrate Your Work

Another symptom of stress is that you underrate your work. In verse 10, Elijah tells God, "I have been very zealous for the Lord God Almighty but the Israelites have rejected your covenant. They have broken down your altar." In other words, "All of my work is in vain. I am the prophet. I have been trying to tell these people to obey the covenant, to worship you, but instead they have broken down the altars. They walk all over the covenant. They don't obey. They have rejected everything. And because they have rejected you, God, they have rejected me."

Under severe stress, you begin to think nothing you do makes a difference. You punch the clock, put in your forty hours, but it doesn't make a difference. You feel that way not only about the job you get paid for, but about the other work you do - your work in the community, your work in the church, your work in your home. You begin to underrate your work and all the good it does.

## Exaggerate Your Problems

A third symptom of stress is that you exaggerate your problems. Elijah goes on to say in verse 10, "I am the only one left. They are trying to kill me too." It is true that Elijah had problems. When a crazy queen and an evil king are trying to kill you, you have a real problem! You exaggerate your problems, but you don't imagine them. Elijah claimed to be the only worshiper of God that was left in Israel. But later on in this story God tells Elijah that there are seven thousand other people who have not bowed to idols. Stress has a way of exaggerating problems in your thinking. The problems get magnified and seem larger and greater than they really are.

## Abdicate Your Dreams

Stress will cause you to abdicate your dreams. In verse four, Elijah says this, "Take my life. I am no better than my ancestors." In other words, "My dreams of making a difference, of being a great spokesman for you, God, are no good. I am no better than anyone before me." Elijah is so stressed out that he has given up on the belief that he can make a difference. He has given up on the great dream that God placed in his heart to make a difference in his country, to be a spokesman for God. He has abdicated his dream.

These are symptoms of stress. When you start depreciating your self worth, when you start underrating the work that you do, when you start exaggerating your problems and making them even worse than they already are, and when you give up and abdicate your dreams, you are suffering from stress.

The life of Elijah shows you that stress was not invented in the last twenty or thirty years. The reality is that the problems that produce stress are universal they just manifest themselves in different situations and circumstances. Elijah's life also shows you some timeless principles that you can apply to overcome stress in your life.

## OVERCOMING STRESS

### Rest Your Body

The first principle is this: to overcome stress you need to rest your body. Elijah had expended a great deal of energy fighting for God. We read that in the desert, "he lay down under the tree and fell asleep. After he rested, an angel touched him and awakened him and told him to get up and eat." In other words, Elijah did not just fall asleep, God allowed him to relax so that he could sleep. You may have had to take sleeping pills, maybe this past week. You may have had to take other kinds of prescription drugs in order to relax enough to be able to rest. God wants you to rest your body. It is good for you to rest and God will help you to rest.

Out in the middle of the desert Elijah found a cake of bread and a jar of water. Where did that cake of bread and jar of water come from? God provided it. God wants to provide for you, He wants you to rest, He wants you to replenish yourself. Overcoming stress begins with resting.

Let me suggest a few little ways you can rest and relax. One is to schedule a few minutes of quiet time in your busy day, a few moments of rest when you don't answer the phone or race from one place to another. For just a few minutes shut your mind off. Even the busiest person can schedule a few minutes. Just take ten minutes. Lie down on the couch in your office or sit back in your chair. Just rest for a few minutes. Give yourself a few quiet moments in the midst of a busy day.

There should be, of course, a more structured planning of restful time. I believe very much in hard work. But as much as I believe in hard work, I am a firm believer in vacations, in taking time to get away. Work hard and play hard is a good plan to follow. A vacation is a time to rest, to forget about your cares. Maybe you have not taken a vacation in a couple of years. You don't think you can afford it. Actually, you can't afford not to if you want to relieve stress. Another way to relax is to do something you find enjoyable and pleasurable. Take in a concert, go to a museum, or take a walk in the woods. Give yourself some breaks from all the difficulty of life. Couples, go out on a date. Sometimes in the busyness of life and family you can go long periods of time without ever doing something together. You can always find an excuse. But you need to take time to go out on a date. Give yourselves some time away to rest and renew yourselves.

## Release Your Frustrations

Another insight we find in Elijah's story is that to cope with stress you need to release your frustrations. Look at what Elijah did. Elijah poured his heart out to God. "I have been zealous," he told God. "I have been working hard for you."

Then he went on to tell God how alone he felt: "I am the only one left. Everybody else has deserted you. I am the only one."

You need to release your frustrations and pour out your heart to God. Holding in your frustrations will only make you sick. Frustrations build and will then manifest themselves in some other, unexpected way.

To release your frustrations, you also need to understand their source. Sometimes the source is unrealistic expectations. One of those is the perfection trap; you think everything has got to be just right, and if it isn't, you are going to go crazy.

But all that thinking does is stress you out. It is not about doing less than your best. But there are times when you get trapped into "everything has got to be perfect" and all that does is make you frustrated and stressed.

You also have to be willing to give up the expectation that life is fair. You are not going to get everything that is supposed to come to you. You have to give up the mentality that "this is what is due me." Because life is not fair. You don't always get what you think is due you. Things don't always turn out the way they are supposed to. Sometimes the referees do blow the game. Sometimes there is not justice in the world. There are times when you can either let this thing destroy you or you can realize that life isn't always fair.

Another way to release your frustrations is to stay in the area of your strengths. When you play to your strengths, you aren't as liable to get frustrated. When you work in the area of your weaknesses, rather than your strengths, you are more apt to be frustrated. If you stay in the area of your strengths and let other people take care of the areas where you are weak, you'll find life more rewarding. When you are working with your gifts and talents, you are not as likely to become stressed out. It is when you are working in an area in which you are not gifted, or doing something you don't feel called to do, that frustration sets in.

## Refocus on God

A third way to cope with stress is this: refocus on God. The Scripture tells us that the Lord spoke to Elijah and said, "Go out and stand on the mountain in the presence of the Lord." Then a great wind blew and an earthquake shook the mountain. Then, after all the violence, there was the gentle voice, the whisper of God's voice. God was getting Elijah focused back on Him.

Sometimes in the midst of the busyness of life with its stress and burdens and pressures, you lose your focus. You need to refocus on God. When you put your focus on God, you see the power of God, the love of God, and the grace of God. When you can get your focus back on God and His greatness, His love for you, His care for you, then your focus is right. When you are out of focus, not focused on God, then stress can build up. Refocusing on God will help you develop a proper perspective on your problems, so that you attack the problem and not the people. When you attack people, you get more problems.

You have got to be able to separate the person from the problem and deal with the issue. It is a matter of perspective.

You refocus on God and develop a proper perspective on life by reading the Bible and spending time in quiet meditation and prayer. When your mind is filled with God's Word and you open yourself to God in prayer, your perspective can change. God changes you. You are renewed and refreshed just by being in the presence of God.

### Resume Serving Others

One final principle for overcoming stress: resume serving others. Later in this story, God tells Elijah, "I want you to go back to Israel. You have a job to do." When you turn the attention away from yourself, your problems and your difficulties, and you look to serve others, you will be surprised what will take place in your life. When you serve others it is amazing how some of those problems take care of themselves. God told Elijah, "I've got a job for you. I'm not finished with you yet." Not only did God send Elijah back to continue the job that He had already given him as a prophet, but He gave him a new job - the job of being the mentor to a young man named Elisha. God wanted Elijah to mentor this young man Elisha because someday he would take his place. If you want to reduce your stress and increase your sense of fulfillment in life, mentor someone else. Pour your life into somebody else's life and help them to develop.

You don't have to be an expert to be a mentor. As a matter of fact, a high school student could mentor a middle high student. A college student could mentor a high school student. Sometimes it is not even a matter of age, it is a matter of experience, knowledge and insight. Part of my role as a pastor is to mentor leaders in the church so that they in turn will mentor other people. Then the leadership will grow and develop, the ministry will expand, and everyone will get the help they need. That is how it is supposed to work. As you serve others, you are able to take your attention off your own problems and difficulties. You also use your God given gifts when you serve which blesses you and those you serve. When you are able to resume your life of service after resting, after releasing your problems, after refocusing your perspective, then you have overcome your stress. The exciting thing is that stress can help you. If you face it and learn how to cope with it, it can help you learn new skills. Skills that you need and there was no other way besides the stress for you to develop them. You can also a gain new direction for your life, as you learn where you need to be going in the days to come.

Stress is a part of life, distress is not. Relieve the distress so that you can have a positive impact on your world.

# BEAT YOUR
# DEPRESSION

In times like these it is very easy to fall into depression. According to the most comprehensive U.S. mental health survey in a decade, almost half of all Americans experience mental illness at some time in their lives and almost a third are afflicted in any one year. The study also found that the most common disorder was a major depressive episode - the exhibition of at least two weeks of symptoms such as low mood and loss of pleasure. I will show you how you can overcome depressive feelings and beat a depressive episode. I will not be giving you the solution for clinical depression. Clinical depression occurs when five or more of the following symptoms are expressed: feelings of sadness and/or irritability; loss of interest or pleasure in activities once enjoyed; changes in weight or appetite; changes in sleep patterns; feelings of guilt, hopelessness, or worthlessness; an inability to concentrate, remember things, or make decisions; fatigue or loss of energy; restlessness or decreased activity noticed by others or thoughts of death or suicide. When one or two of these symptoms are present that indicates a depressive episode or depressive feelings, but when five or more are present that is clinical depression. A more serious and weighty issue than we can discuss here and one that requires professional help. All of us have either struggled or will struggle with depressive feelings or depressive episodes. This is because of all the bad things that happen in this world; there are so many problems, so many difficulties and our world is so complex. Almost all of us are touched by sin, hurt, violence, rejection and other things that are beyond our control. Sometimes we find ourselves in situations where we try to do the right thing, yet things do not work out. Jeremiah was someone like this, a man who had a very clear sense of purpose, but found that things did not work out whatever he did. It caused him to be depressed, as we see in Jeremiah 20:7-12, "0 Lord, You deceived me and I was deceived; You overpowered me and prevailed. I am ridiculed all day long; everyone mocks me. Whenever I speak, I cry out proclaiming violence and destruction. So the word of the Lord has brought me insult and reproach all day long. But if I say, 'I will not mention Him or speak any more in His name,' His word is in my heart like a fire, a fire shut up in my bones. I am weary of holding it in; indeed, I cannot. I hear many whispering, Terror on every side! Report him! Let's report him!' All my friends are waiting for me to slip, saying, 'Perhaps he will be deceived; then we will prevail over him and take our revenge on him.' But the Lord is with me like a mighty warrior; so my persecutors will stumble and not prevail. They will fail and be thoroughly disgraced; their dishonor will never be forgotten. 0 Lord Almighty, You who examine the righteous and probe the heart and mind, let me see Your vengeance upon them, for to You I have committed my cause. Sing to the Lord! Give praise to the Lord!

He rescues the life of the needy from the hands of the wicked."

## CAUSES OF DEPRESSION

### Frustration

There are a few causes for depression. The first cause of depression is frustration. Jeremiah was frustrated because he felt that God had deceived him. God gave him something to say and he assumed that if he followed God's will, the outcome would be positive. Have you ever been in a situation like that, where you have a goal and you strive to achieve that goal because you believe it is a good thing, but then it doesn't seem to work? It is frustrating! Now, a little bit of frustration is part of life, but when we continually beat our heads against the wall, it eventually starts to hurt. When I was young and just learning to ride a bike, I decided to swap bikes with my sister and try one of those "girl bikes." I jumped on her bike and started going down the hill next to our home. At the bottom of the hill was a parking lot and through the parking lot was a very large stone church. I don't know exactly what happened, but I could not seem to figure out how to stop that bike, so I smashed right into the large stone church. I will tell you that it hurt a whole lot and I got a bump on my head that looked like something from a cartoon. In life, we may not have any physical stone walls, but we can find ourselves hitting serious barriers nevertheless. This is frustrating and frustration can develop and lead to depression.

## Rejection

Later, Jeremiah says, "I am ridiculed all day long, everyone mocks me." When we are rejected by the people who are important to us, it can hit so deep that it can lead to depression. We begin to wonder about our lives, our futures, and we feel hopeless because there is nothing left to anticipate. Rejection is difficult for anyone to handle regardless of the situation, but when we experience repeated rejections over a period of time, this leads us to a place of depression.

## Anxiety

We see in verse 10 that Jeremiah's heart was gripped with fear because he was surrounded by people waiting for him to make a mistake; even his friends were waiting to rejoice in his failures. In that mode of fear, our minds can play tricks on us and begin to create anxieties and fears that might not exist, this kind of fear can bring on depressive feelings. We wonder why we are so lethargic, have no energy, and have lost interest in things we previously enjoyed. That kind of depression makes it difficult to feel motivated to do anything at all.

These causes of depression finally led Jeremiah to ask God, "Why did you even let me be born?" I want to share an important truth with you: Life is difficult. There are not always answers to our problems and we can't fix everything. When life is bad; we feel down, grieve our losses, and experience the gloom of depression. You may think that those who follow Christ are not supposed to be depressed, but that is not true, depression and grief are normal human reactions. Christ followers should not remain depressed, but they can certainly be depressed.

Jeremiah responded to his depression with the words: "I would rather not have lived if I have to live this way." Still today, some people respond to depression with suicidal thoughts. Others respond with a spending spree, or an eating binge, or getting drunk or high on drugs. Of course, after the binge or the spree is over, the depression is deepened because there are now consequences which must be dealt with. These kinds of responses to depression can never help, they only make things worse.

These are some of the issues involved in depression, and if we respond to depressive feelings in a negative way, we create an environment which only causes more depression. Then how do we beat depression?

## BEATING DEPRESSION

### Discern The Seasons Of Life

The first thing Jeremiah did to help him deal with depression was discern the seasons of life. God has seasons of life for us just like there are seasons in nature. There is Winter, when it seems there is no growth and everything is barren. There is Spring, a season of planting without seeing any results. There is Summer, a season of great activity and effort. There is Fall, when we are able to bring in a harvest and see the results of our labor. We would like to live in such a season all the time, but we can't always live in a time of harvest, because in order to harvest we must first plant. And we must remember that without Winter, there won't be a good harvest the following year. It is normal to have depressive feelings in a winter season when we experience loss.

If you lose a loved one, a job, or anything precious to you, you should feel grief and depression. This week marks the two year anniversary of my mother's death. I can tell you when you lose someone so close to you depressive feelings will surely come.

God told Jeremiah that, "Before you were ever born, I picked you to be a spokesman for me." That's a pretty impressive way to begin your life! Jeremiah prophesied for God, but his words didn't come true and everyone ridiculed and laughed at him. He prophesied this way for years, until finally his Fall season came and things began to happen. Everything he had prophesied came true, so he was able to realize that things had been working out the way they were supposed to all along, but he had to pass through the other seasons first. We need to develop discernment so we can see where we are in our lives. We can't always be in harvest time, but the good news is that Winter does not last forever, Spring follows with new life, new opportunities, and new hopes.

## Understand God Is Always At Work

In order to defeat depression, we also must understand that God is at work even when He seems silent. Even when God does not seem to be doing anything; He is examining, probing, and working around our world. He cares even when we accuse Him of neglect. We can express our feelings to God, it won't bother Him or hurt His feelings if we tell Him how lousy our lives are and why we think it is all His fault. In fact, the best thing you can do is pour your heart out to God, the best thing to do for a depressed person is allow them to express their feelings.

We also see in the Scripture that Jeremiah challenged God's character, saying, "0 Lord you deceived me." But he also realized that in the end God will bring justice, even if it is not on our timeline. We feel that we need everything now, but God does not work that way. We may think God is silent, but then we realize that He has been working in us and changing us all along. Your perspective on a situation changes, or you grow a little more which proves that God has been at work .

## Praise God Anyway

Another way to beat depression is to praise God in spite of your situation and circumstances. You may wonder how you can praise Him in the midst of your rejections and frustrations? You can always praise Him because you have hope in God's faithfulness. Faithfulness is God's very nature, it is impossible for Him to be unfaithful. You can know that even when everybody else gives up on you and hurts you, that God will never leave or forsake you. You can't go too far or sink too low because wherever you are, He will be there too. You need to be able to praise God even in tough times. You will be surprised at how God works in your life through your difficulties.

Many years ago there was a lawyer in the Midwest who fell into such a terrible depression that his friends came into his home and removed all the knives and razors because they feared he might try to kill himself. In the midst of this depression he wrote, "I am the most miserable man living. Whether I shall ever be better, I cannot tell. I awfully forebode I shall not." Yet God helped him through his depressive episode and this man went on to become the greatest president our country has ever known: Abraham Lincoln.

# DON'T LET DOUBT DEFEAT YOU

How can you overcome doubt to make sure doubt does not defeat you? In II Corinthians 4:8 it says, "We are often troubled but not crushed, sometimes in doubt but never in despair. There are many enemies but we are never without a friend and though we badly hurt at times we are not destroyed." I believe that our society has created a kind of doubting person because there are so many phrases that we all know. We all know the one called Murphy's Law. Murphy's Law goes like this, "If anything can go wrong, it will." Now that is not a positive thing to say, that is a doubting thing to say. There are some other laws, I don't know if you have ever heard of the names but I believe you have heard these phrases. Finagle's Law goes like this, "Once a job is fouled up anything done to improve it will only make it worse." Or how about Chism's Law which says, "Any time things appear to be getting better you have overlooked something." Everywhere we turn there are messages of doubt so it is easy for doubt to defeat us.

When we look at the Scripture it is so important where it says "sometimes in doubt but never in despair." The doubts may come and we will look at the causes but we don't have to be in despair. We don't have to be despondent; though the doubts may come the despair does not have to happen.

## CAUSES OF DOUBT

### Criticism

What are some of the causes of doubt? I think the first is

criticism. There is a quote that I keep close to my desk that goes like this, "To escape criticism, do nothing, say nothing, be nothing." You cannot escape criticism; you cannot accomplish things in life without encountering criticism. As a matter of fact, the higher up you go in leadership the more the criticism comes. You look at the president of the United States; he gets criticized from every direction. The governor, the mayor, the teacher, the coach, the pastor all get their share of criticism. The higher you go, the more you open yourself up to criticism. If you want to do something with your life the criticism is going to come and you need to be ready for it. You need to know it is going to come so you don't let that criticism cause you begin to doubt yourself. You can't feel good about life when you doubt yourself, your decisions and your actions.

## Circumstances

Another cause of doubt is circumstances. There are circumstances that take place in life when bad things happen. Bad things sometimes happen and the circumstances are sometimes beyond your control. When this happens the doubts begin to flood in and you begin to doubt yourself, you begin to doubt your purpose in life, you begin to doubt who you are. You question whether you are fulfilling God's plan for your life. You wonder whether you can achieve your dreams and see good things happen in your life. Thomas Edison was such a great inventor and he invented so many fascinating things but along the away he had a lot of disappointments. One time he had just completed another failed attempt at a filament that would make the light bulb work and he came inside and his wife said, "Aren't you pretty discouraged, Tom." His answer was, "Certainly not, now I know ten thousand ways it does not work." That is a marvelous way to deal with your doubts. Understand that your experience has taught you what does not work so you refocus on a new and better approach.

## What Doubt Does

### Blows Everything Out Of Proportion

Those are two causes for doubt but it is what doubt does that can cause you to not feel good about your life. The first thing doubt does is it blows everything out of proportion. You begin to look at circumstances, you begin to look at your critics and they look bigger than they really are. All of the sudden something, which is not really that big, becomes a mountain to you. This is what doubt can do to you; it can mess with your mind. It can get you to think things that aren't really true and if they are true they are certainly not as big or as monumental as you make them out to be.

### Creates Uncertainty In Your Mind

The second thing that doubt can do is it can create uncertainty in your mind when you need to make some very critical and important decisions. Doubt has a way of doing this to you right when you need so much to be able to make a good decision. Those nagging doubts can overwhelm you and if you are not careful you can make a decision in a doubting frame of mind instead of a believing frame of mind. Then you make a bad decision and that bad decision creates worse circumstances, which then creates - more doubt. If you get wrapped up in that cycle, you are going from doubt to despair to bad decisions to more doubt and more despair.

## Becomes Contagious

Another thing doubt can do is to become contagious. I believe when you are around doubting people it spreads and I think that when you are around believing people that spreads too. I don't know if you know where that phrase "doubting Thomas" comes from but it actually comes from a story in the Bible about a disciple of Jesus named Thomas. When Jesus had risen from the grave and came to see his disciples Thomas just could not believe it was really Jesus. So he actually asked Jesus to see his hands. He needed to see the evidence before he could believe Jesus had been resurrected. When you are around the kind of people that say things like, "let me see," "how do you know?," "are you sure?" that doubting can be very contagious. Around those kinds of people, it can be easy to begin to move from belief to doubt.

## Limits God

I think that doubt limits God. You may think that God cannot be limited but He actually can. Jesus said, "I can do no miracle working here because of the unbelief." Jesus had all the power to do miracles and He did many but in that place the doubt limited what He could do. Doubting limits the power of God in your life and you need the power of God. There are challenges in life, there are things which you face every day that can defeat you. In order to not be defeated you need the power of God. When you limit God's power because of doubt you are hurting yourself. You are letting doubt defeat you.

### Limits Your Potential

Not only does doubt limit God it also limits your potential. To feel good about your life you need to reach your full potential. You can never reach your potential if you allow doubt to win in your life. You can never be the winner that God has destined you to be if you allow doubt to constantly come in to your life and overwhelm your mind. Doubt keeps you from enjoying life. Doubt does bad things to a person but how do you overcome it?

## YOU CAN DEFEAT DOUBT

### Don't Rely On Yourself

You can defeat doubt. You begin by understanding that doubt

can remind you that you are relying on yourself. The first thing you need to remember about doubt is that doubt may actually be reminding you that you are relying too much on yourself. There was someone in the Bible who had this happen to him and his name was Moses. He started doubting God's power and this is someone who had seen God work and had seen the power of God, yet he began to doubt it. The reason he doubted is because he was relying on himself instead of on God. If you are relying only on yourself, on your abilities, on your intellect, on your savvy to get you through life then you are going to experience doubts. You cannot make it on your own but if you have the power of God working in your life that turns everything around. If you are doing it on your own, you are probably going to doubt, if you are doing it with the power of God you don't have to doubt.

People and circumstances have a way of controlling your life if you let them. What you need to do is let God control your life. When you let people, when you let opinions, when you let circumstances control your life what happens is you are always questioning and second-guessing yourself. When you let God control, when you follow God's plan for your life, it feels good.

## Admit Doubt

Another way to defeat doubt is to admit doubt. Occasional doubts are part of being human. It is okay to doubt and in fact some pretty important people have doubted from time to time. Job found himself really wondering about God and his life. John the Baptist had his doubts about Jesus. Sometimes we do doubt, sometimes we do find ourselves in positions where a little doubt kind of creeps in. It is not a matter of never having doubt; it is a matter of what you do with those doubts. Admitting doubt actually helps to overcome doubts. When you admit the doubt you begin to put life in proper perspective, you begin to see things the way they really are. And you open the door for God to work.

There is a story of a famous Christian from England whose

name was George Mueller. He established orphanages and he was on a trip from England to Canada when a heavy fog came over the ocean and the whole ship, the captain and all the stewards got very nervous because they were afraid that they were going to crash into another ship. They were also afraid that they might crash into an iceberg. In the midst of all this, George Mueller came up on deck and he told the captain that he needed to be in Toronto by Sunday. The captain responded by indicating they were in trouble and Mueller's speaking schedule was not high on the list of priorities. Mueller said that he had been in the ministry for forty years and had never missed a speaking engagement and did not want to miss one now. He decided to pray and encouraged the captain to come with him. They went down in the ship and they began to pray and George Mueller was admitting his doubts but was praying for God's intervention and then when he was done the captain felt obligated to pray. After a short while George Mueller tapped him on the shoulder and told him to stop praying because he could tell the captain did not believe a word he was praying. Mueller told the captain he doubted but yet believed in God's power and when they walked back to the deck the fog had cleared.

God is all-powerful; He is a miracle working God. We function in the natural and God functions in the supernatural. Things that are impossible with man or not impossible with God. In your human intellect you may have some doubts but you need to remind yourself that you serve a God who can do the impossible.

### Practice The Principle Of Replacement

A third way to defeat doubt is to practice the principle of replacement. The principle of replacement works like this: instead of saying "I can't," you say "I can," instead of saying 'if," you say 'I will," instead of saying "I don't think," you say "I know," instead of saying "I don't have time," you say "I will make the time," instead of saying "maybe," you say "positively," instead of saying, "I'm afraid," you say "I'm confident," instead of saying "I don't believe," you say "I believe," instead of saying, "it's impossible," you say "God is able." Practice the principle of replacement from the negative to the positive and your doubts will disappear. You may think is this just some sort of power of positive speech but this is the power of possibility thinking. This is the power of believing that you don't have to stay here in your life when God wants you over there. It is replacing doubt with the truth of the Bible which says in Philippians 4:13, "I can do all things through Christ who empowers me."

## Expect Good Things To Happen
## And Act Upon Them

The next way to defeat doubt is to expect good things to happen and act upon them. Sometimes you are in doubt because you are not expecting anything to happen. You need to get a dream of how good your life can be. As long as you dwell on your problems or long for the ways things used to be you have no expectation of a better future. Expect to get a new job, expect to start a new relationship, expect to get the break you need to feel good about life again. You need to get something in your heart and you need to start acting on that. The doubts will begin to go away and the negative will be filled with the positive. Expect good things to happen but don't just expect it, act upon it.

## Resist Doubt

A final way to defeat doubt is to resist it. Resist doubt and practice trusting God. This is something that takes practice. Because you just don't all of a sudden completely achieve trust in God. There are many things that keep happening in your life and you have to keep resisting the doubts and keep trusting in God. What is important to remember is that God loves you, God believes in you and God wants to bless you. God believes in you so you need to believe in yourself. God knows you, He has given you gifts, and He has given you dreams. Put your trust in Him, don't allow the doubts to come in and stay. Here is a motto I came across years ago which comes from Robert Schuller, "Whatever the mind can conceive and I will dare to believe, with God's help, I can achieve."

# ANGER: LIVE WITH IT OR WITHOUT IT

The reality is that all of us face situations and challenges that may make us angry, no one is immune. When the famous painter Leonardo da Vinci was painting The Last Supper, he became angry with someone impeding his progress and lashed out at them. After that incident, he went back to his painting but when he reached the point of painting the face of Jesus he found that he could not do it without first making things right with the person who had caused his anger. Regardless of our emotional makeup, anger affects all of us and when we allow anger to control us, we feel poorly knowing that we must make things right.

Several years ago, Temple University lost a basketball game to the University of Massachusetts by one point. John Chaney, the Temple coach, stormed into the press conference after the game and lashed out at John Calipari, the coach of the University of Massachusetts. He ended his tirade with the words, "I am going to kill you!" and he did it right in front of all the microphones. That outburst of anger cost John Chaney dearly: his wife left him, his daughter wouldn't even speak to him, and he was suspended by the University. He found that the repercussions for allowing anger to get the best of him were serious. Anger grips our lives and causes us to do things we later wish we had not done.

## Anger Is Acceptable

The Bible tells us in Ephesians 4:26-27, "In your anger do not sin. Do not let the sun go down while you are still angry. Do not give the devil a foothold." This tells you something very important, that it is acceptable to be angry. God never told you not to be angry as a matter of fact, even Jesus got angry. In John 2:13 it says, "He went to the temple where He saw tables set up for buying and selling, like a business. He became angry when He saw that the temple, which should have been a place of prayer and worship. had been converted to a business." Jesus overturned the tables and made everyone leave because He was angry, but He did not sin in His anger. Further, Mark 3:5 says, speaking of Jesus, "He looked around at them in anger, deeply distressed at their stubborn hearts." It is okay to be angry, anger is an emotion, it is a feeling. To suppress the feelings and emotions that God created in you is unhealthy because that repression of anger will always express itself somewhere in some way.

The constructive expression of anger can even be helpful. If you can communicate to another person that something they have said or done has been hurtful, then maybe you can change the situation or the person so that you are not hurt again. If you cannot communicate your hurt and anger, you will find yourself in the same circumstances over and over, you need to break the cycle by dealing with your anger.

## Unresolved Anger Causes Problems

Another insight about anger is that unresolved anger causes problems. Verse 27 says, "Do not give the devil a foothold." The word for foothold means "a place," or "an opportunity." You can't give the devil an opportunity or a foothold where he can get into your life. Unresolved anger gives the enemy an opportunity to lead you into unkind thoughts, actions, and words, all of which have consequences.

Unresolved anger can even cause health problems. The University of Tennessee completed a study on women and anger in which they discovered that many health problems, such as depression, headaches, obesity and autoimmune diseases are the direct results of allowing unresolved anger to fester. Such anger-related illness is more common in women because men are more likely to express their anger. The reality is that many times your anger stems from unrealistic expectations which you place on yourself. You become angry when you cannot change frustrating circumstances at work, when family members, friends, and co-workers fail to live up to your expectations, or when you believe you are being treated unfairly or disrespectfully. The anger triggered by these things is normal, it is what happens if the anger goes unresolved that can cause problems. The circumstances and consequences of unresolved anger affect all our lives, even though we try to go through life avoiding the subject.

I spent a good part of my young life being taught to use my anger to achieve better athletic performance but when I stopped playing sports, I had to enter the real world and it is not always easy to make the switch. Frankly, it is most difficult to do this in the privacy of our own homes when our guard is at its lowest point. Sometimes the worst outbursts of anger take place among those we care about most, this is unfortunate but true.

## Types of Anger

There are different types of anger, psychologists generally divide them into four categories. The first of these is passive anger, this is when you say, "Oh, don't mind me, go ahead and have fun. I'll just stay home and watch TV." The second type is aggressive anger, the one you are probably most familiar with when someone becomes aggressive and shouts or maybe even gets physical. There is no question they are angry. There is also passive aggressive anger, when somebody chronically comes late or overspends, or in some way causes problems for others. The expression of anger is passive, yet the anger is certainly present, you can be angry without yelling or screaming or hitting somebody. The final type of anger is indirect anger, which occurs when we use a third person to express our anger at someone else - that third party may be a child or someone else in the family. Regardless of its manifestation anger touches all of our lives, men and women, young and old and is not something we can avoid by moving or changing. Anger is an emotion that is in our world and in our lives, the question then is what can we do about it?

## Deal With Your Anger

Verse 26 says, "Do not let the sun go down while you are still angry," which simply means deal with your anger. It is acceptable to be angry but we must deal with our anger to avoid the problems caused when anger remains unresolved. My wife and I took this particular scripture to heart when we got married making a covenant that we would never go to bed at night and still be angry with each other. We have had a few discussions that have taken us early into the morning, but it has worked for us. There are ways of dealing with anger.

## Clarify The Issue

The first way to deal with anger is to clarify the real issue by asking yourself what really made you angry. If there is an argument over what color the curtains should be, you need to realize that color is probably not the real issue. It may be anything from how much the curtains cost to who gets to make the decision. Additionally, many times when you are upset, you may take your anger out on people who are not part of the real issue. It is important to clarify the real reason for anger. To do this, you may have to dig deep and give yourself time to really think about everything that has happened. Sometimes you may have to trace back through your whole day to find out what first made you angry because the manifestation was taking place throughout the day, but the anger began with a specific incident.

### Give Yourself Time

The second way to deal with anger is to give yourself time. This can be an enormous challenge because many times we express anger in the heat of the moment. If you can detach yourself from the situation for a moment, you will be less likely to say or do something you would regret later. You get mad and just blow up, then you have to deal with that explosion and its consequences because you just let your anger take control. This has certainly been the case in my life - I have come a long way, but I know that I still have a long way to go. And I have learned that taking some time can really help to diffuse a situation and allow enough time to deal with things in a healthy and rational manner. You must be smarter than to let the anger take over, so you must give yourself time.

## Keep Up Communication

The third way to deal with anger is to keep an door open for communication to take place. Alexander the Great was an incredible strategist and soldier. At one time one of his boyhood friends who had been promoted to general in his army, was drunk and began to speak disrespectfully to Alexander. In a fit of anger Alexander grabbed his spear and threw it at his friend. His intent was simply to scare his friend, but his aim was poor and he hit his friend in the heart killing him instantly. This great man who was able to conquer nations could not conquer his own anger; as a result he lost one of his dear friends. He was so distraught that he wept for days and even tried to kill himself.

One thing that can be helpful if it is difficult to communicate verbally, is to communicate in written form. You can use paper or email to get your thoughts in order so you say what really needs to be said. Sometimes people may use memos because they lack the courage to speak to someone directly, this only creates anger. What you need to do is take some time, calm down, and put your thoughts in writing. It is hard sometimes to tell someone how very hurtful their actions were and it may be easier to put it down on paper. This opens up communication in a surprising way and as long as people are communicating, there is hope for healing and restoration. When people stop talking, problems inevitably follow.

## Understand Levels of Anger

Finally, maybe the most helpful way to overcome anger is to learn how to use degrees of anger. If someone in a movie theater is making noise behind you, you could turn around, dump their popcorn over their head and tell them to shut up. Or you could politely turn around and ask them to be quiet, most people will stop then out of sheer embarrassment. If the problem continues though, you could ask them again to be quiet and you could move from there to calling the ushers or the manager. The benefit of this type of approach is that instead of a quick escalation of anger there are steps, and you will find that many things can get resolved along the way. Sometimes when we get angry, we just jump over all of these and nobody can understand what our problem is, but if we go level by level, step by step, everyone will know why we are angry.

We live in what has been called "The Age of Rage." America is the most violent country in the world, for every homicide in

England, there are thirteen in America. Several years ago, Jack Nicholson was cut off on the highway, so he got out of his car and smashed the man's Mercedes with a crowbar. Violence affects everyone in this age and people just explode. The Christian lifestyle is different and one of the ways to show that difference is by not allowing anger to control you. The reality is that there will be times when you are in situations over which you have no control. When this happens, you must be willing to acknowledge you don't control this situation and getting angry is not going to do any good. In fact, it will likely make things worse. In a society where rage is everywhere, people are responding negatively to the economy. It does not mean you are above the temptation, or that you have stopped ever being angry. Remember, even Jesus got angry. It is when anger goes unresolved, that problems develop.

Frederick Buechner said, speaking about anger, "To lick your wounds, to smack your lips over grievances long past, to savor to the last tooth some morsel both the pain you have been given and the pain you are giving back in many ways is a feast fit for a king. The chief drawback is that while you are wolfing down, you are wolfing down yourself. The skeleton at the feast is you." In the end anger hurts you more than it does anybody else, you destroy only yourself. God does not want that for you because He has something much better planned for your life.

# STOP WORRYING: START LIVING

According to Harper's Index, the average American is in a bad mood 110 days out of the year. That means that for about 30% of the time, people are in a bad mood because of things like anger and stress and what we will focus on in this chapter - worry.

In Matthew 6:25-34 Jesus said: "Therefore, I tell you do not worry about your life, what you will eat or drink; or about your body, what you will wear. Is not life more important than food, and the body more important than clothes? Look at the birds of the air; they do not sow or reap or store away in barns, and yet your heavenly Father feeds them. Are you not much more valuable than they? Who of you by worrying can add a single hour to his life? And why do you worry about clothes? See how the lilies of the field grow. They do not labor or spin. Yet I tell you that not even Solomon in all his splendor was dressed like one of these. If that is how God clothes the grass of the field, which is here today and tomorrow thrown into the fire, will he not much more clothe you, 0 you of little faith? So do not worry, saying "What shall we eat?" of "What shall we drink?" or "What shall we wear?" For the pagans run after all these things, and your heavenly Father knows that you need them. But seek first His kingdom and His righteousness, and all these things will be given to you as well. Therefore do not worry about tomorrow, for tomorrow will worry about itself. Each day has enough trouble of its own."

You may know the story of Olympic speed skater Dan Jansen. Considered one of the best speed skaters in the world, Jansen competed in three Olympics without ever winning a medal. In observing his career and listening to interviews, you can see that he was burdened throughout his career by worry. In his first Olympics, his sister died just before he skated. In Albertville, France he had the pressure of knowing that he held the world record and was the favorite to win. Two years later he set a new world record two weeks before Olympic competition. Remember, the Olympics is different from basketball, football, and other sports. When Jansen didn't win in the Olympics that represented four years of training without winning the biggest reward. His last opportunity to win Olympic gold came in the 1000 meter race. He was not the favorite in this race because his specialty was the 500 meter race, so he was able to be more relaxed. As a result when he slipped during the race, instead of overcompensating, he relaxed and made his way around the turn to the finish line. He finally won his first gold medal, even setting a new world record in the process. When Jansen stopped worrying, he finally got the gold medal he richly deserved.

WORRY IS...

## Irreverent

Some basic understanding about worry needs to be established before worry can be overcome. The first is that worry is irreverent because it fails to recognize that God is working in this world. God is in control - He has not forgotten you and placed you in exile somewhere. God is at work, doing new things all the time, but when you worry, you are saying that God is not in control. And worry is disobedient to God because He commands you not to worry.

## Irresponsible

Worry is irresponsible because it wastes your energy so that you don't have the energy you need for constructive and creative problem solving. It is irresponsible to feel that you are responsible for other peoples happiness (spouse, children, friends, co-workers.)

Worry wears you out and burdens you so that you don't have what is needed to know how to overcome situations in your life.

## Irrelevant

A third thing to note is that worry is irrelevant, it cannot change anything. Worry accomplishes nothing beneficial. It is not constructive but destructive, it is not a help but a hindrance, it is not part of the solution but part of the problem. Experts have estimated that forty percent of things you worry about will never even happen, thirty percent of things you worry about are things from the past, twelve percent of your worries are about your health (when nothing is actually wrong with you), and ten percent of things you worry about are too petty and insignificant to really affect your future. That means that only eight percent of the things you worry about legitimately deserve your concern and thought. Worry is irrelevant, irresponsible and irreverent, and does an enormous amount of harm. Modern medical research has shown that worry can break down your resistance to disease and can cause medical problems in the digestive organs and the heart. So, how can you overcome worry?

## OVERCOMING WORRY

### Trust God

To overcome worry you must trust God for the things that are beyond your control. As long as you are in control of a situation you feel safe and secure, but when there are issues beyond your control you begin to worry. This past year I experienced first hand how powerful the pull of worry can be. I have been practicing for years the principles I am sharing with you but events transpired that caused me to fall into serious worry. I found myself going through possible scenarios while I could not sleep at night. I would find that a particular subject I read or something I would hear caused me to go into the same worry scenarios. Whenever my mind was not occupied my thoughts would drift toward worry about these different issues. The result was that I began to suffer physically and emotionally. It was a terrible time in my life and reemphasized for me that you cannot feel good about life when you worry. You want to control everything about your life, but you can't because there will always be things that are beyond your control. Nothing is more painful to me personally than listening to people look back into their past regretting events and wishing that things had been different. You need to be in control of the things that you have the ability to control, but you need to trust God for the rest.

When you start to feel anxious, you need to avoid panic by giving your burden to God in prayer. How can you trust God? By learning His promises. There are over 7,000 promises found in the Bible. Take stock of your thought life. Review what you have been thinking and what thoughts you have been listening to. God has promised you all kinds of marvelous things and the best thing you can do is begin to learn those promises. You need to give your needs to God in prayer, trusting that He will take care of you and believing in His promises; when you do this you also learn to trust Him more. And you don't need to worry when you can trust God for the things that are beyond your control.

## Put God First

Another way to overcome worry is to put God first in your life. Jesus told you to seek first His kingdom and His righteousness and all of these things would be given to you. You must get your priorities in proper order. God needs to be first, family second and your career third. If you let the wrong priority be first it will create an enormous amount of worry in your life. When you put God first, it is amazing what will happen. This does not mean that family and work are not important, to avoid planning for your family or to ignore what the boss thinks or how the company is doing would be foolish and irresponsible.

In Matthew 6:24, Jesus says that "No one can serve two

masters because either they will hate the one or love the other." Essentially, Jesus is saying that you can't serve both God and money. For many this is where putting God first really is revealed. When your finances begin to get shaky, the issue of who and what you serve needs to be settled once and for all. Jesus is not saying if you serve God you will be poor, it means simply that you can't serve two masters and you must decide what your priorities will be. When you put God first you won't worry as much because when you get your eyes on God, you will find encouragement. He will build you up, strengthening you so that you can walk in a confidence that is rooted completely in who God is. When you put God in the first position, He will change your thinking and rid you of the burdensome worries and the petty things that have no place in your life. Jesus asks you, "If you worry, is it going to add anything to your life?" The answer is no, but worry can take many things away from you. You won't be healthy, you won't live as long and you will be unable to have a happy life. A simple motto "Don't worry, Be Happy" is not the answer. When you put God first you will find that you will worry less and you will be a lot happier.

## Take Life As It Comes

The third principle for overcoming worry is take life as it comes, one day at a time. Jesus said, "Don't worry about tomorrow because tomorrow will worry about itself. Each day has enough trouble of its own." He is telling you to take life one day at a time and not look into the future asking "what if?" Most worries revolve around dwelling on what we don't know. That kind of thinking will do nothing but prevent you from having the boldness to step out and do the things that God wants you to do today. You may have some great dreams for fantastic things that you want to do, but you can so easily be held back by worry about the future.

I believe in planning for the future and in setting goals, but I don't believe in worrying about the future. Too often as adults we forget that we still need the dreams and the goals that we had as children, especially when the worries start to enter our lives. You need to decide between the 90-10 rule and the 10-90 rule. The 90-10 rule is when you worry about the problem 90% of the time and try to figure out how to solve it 10% of the time. The 10-90 rule is when you worry about the problem 10% of the time and spend 90% of your creative intellectual energy trying to find out solutions. The 10-90 rule will put you farther down the road to your goals.

Fog can blanket a city for seven blocks and be as much as 100 feet deep. Fog that thick can cause you to stop moving forward since you can't see in front of you. But if you were to take that fog and change it into water, it would only fill up a single glass. Worry can be like this - a giant that is seven blocks wide and 100 feet deep. But when you see it for what it really is, you see that it is nothing more than a glass of water. With God on your side, you can overcome whatever the challenge is that causes you to worry. God does not want you just to make it through this life until you get to Heaven - He wants you to feel good about life...again

# ABOUT THE AUTHOR

**Rick McDaniel** is the founder and senior pastor of Richmond Community Church, a contemporary multi-site church located in Richmond, Virginia. He is also the speaker on High Impact Living where his audio messages can be heard on audible.com and his video messages can be viewed on amazon.com. Rick has three earned degrees including an advanced degree from Duke University and has also written three books. He has spoken around the world on five continents to thousands of people. Rick has been married to his wife Michelle for 27 years and has two sons Matt and Wes.

Made in the USA